Fundraising
at School

By Heather Hammonds

T0342764

Contents

Fundraising

Fundraising is a way to raise money, or funds, to help others.

Money is sometimes raised at school.

Money collected through fundraising can help schools, sports groups, charity groups or other people who need money.

A walkathon is a way to raise money.
Many people can take part in a walkathon.

Children and teachers can organise a walkathon.
All children can take part in the walkathon
to help raise money.

Teachers can buy sports equipment,
or other things for the school,
with the money that is raised.

A readathon is a way to raise money. Children read many different books when they take part in a readathon.

Children and teachers can organise a readathon.
All children can take part in the readathon
to help raise money.

Teachers can buy books
or other things for the school library,
with the money that is raised.

A spellathon is a way to raise money.
Children learn to spell many words
in a spellathon.

A class at school can hold a spellathon.
Children receive money for each word
they spell correctly.

Fundraising is a very good way
for children and teachers
to raise money for their school or for charity.

Spellathon

Goal

To organise a spellathon at school to raise money.

Materials

You will need:

- a list of twenty words for each child

- sponsor forms

- sponsors

- pencils

- paper.

1.   Decide what you are going to raise money for.

2. Ask your teacher to help each child make a list of twenty words to learn during the spellathon.

3. Make a sponsor form.

Sponsor's name
Mum and Dad
Grandma
Cameron Witt
Sarah Watson
Aunty Kate
Jessica Hart
Antony Davidson

4. Tell your parents about the spellathon, then ask family and friends to be your sponsors.

ount per word	Total
$1	
$2	
50c	
50c	
$2	
50c	
40c	
Total donations	

5. Ask your teacher to give the class a spelling test.

6. Ask your teacher to mark the spelling tests carefully.

7. Count all the words you spelt correctly.

8. Collect the money from your sponsors.

9. Give the money to your teacher.